BE A MAKER!

Maker Projects for Kids Who Love
GREENING UP SPACES

MEGAN KOPP

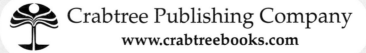

Crabtree Publishing Company
www.crabtreebooks.com

Crabtree Publishing Company

www.crabtreebooks.com

Author: Megan Kopp

Series research and development: Reagan Miller

Editors: Sarah Eason, and Philip Gebhardt

Proofreader: Wendy Scavuzzo

Editorial director: Kathy Middleton

Design: Paul Myerscough

Layout: Simon Borrough

Cover design: Paul Myerscough

Photo research: Rachel Blount

**Production coordinator
and prepress technician:** Tammy McGarr

Print coordinator: Margaret Amy Salter

Consultant: Jennifer Turliuk, CEO MakerKids

Production coordinated by Calcium Creative

Library and Archives Canada Cataloguing in Publication

Kopp, Megan, author
    Maker projects for kids who love greening up spaces
/ Megan Kopp.

(Be a maker!)
Includes index.
Issued in print and electronic formats.
ISBN 978-0-7787-2881-8 (hardcover).--
ISBN 978-0-7787-2895-5 (softcover).--
ISBN 978-1-4271-1911-7 (HTML)

    1. Gardening--Juvenile literature. I. Title. II.
Series: Be a maker!

SB457.K67 2017   j635   C2016-907378-5
                                C2016-907379-3

Library of Congress Cataloging-in-Publication Data

Names: Kopp, Megan, author.
Title: Maker projects for kids who love greening up spaces /
  Megan Kopp.
Other titles: Be a maker!
Description: New York, New York : Crabtree Publishing
  Company, [2017] |
  Series: Be a maker! | Includes index.
Identifiers: LCCN 2016050631 (print) | LCCN 2016052603 (ebook)
  ISBN 9780778728818 (reinforced library binding) |
  ISBN 9780778728955 (pbk.) |
  ISBN 9781427119117 (Electronic HTML)
Subjects: LCSH: Gardening--Juvenile literature.
Classification: LCC SB457 .K67 2017 (print) | LCC SB457 (ebook)
  | DDC 635--dc23
LC record available at https://lccn.loc.gov/2016050631

Crabtree Publishing Company

www.crabtreebooks.com   1-800-387-7650

Printed in Canada/022017/CH20161214

Published in Canada
Crabtree Publishing
616 Welland Ave.
St. Catharines, Ontario
L2M 5V6

Published in the United States
Crabtree Publishing
PMB 59051
350 Fifth Avenue, 59th Floor
New York, New York 10118

Published in the United Kingdom
Crabtree Publishing
Maritime House
Basin Road North, Hove
BN41 1WR

Published in Australia
Crabtree Publishing
3 Charles Street
Coburg North
VIC, 3058

CONTENTS

MAKE IT GREEN!

From an apartment balcony to a patch of earth in the backyard—almost any space can be made green! Landscaping is the hands-on act of combining plants and other materials to make a space more beautiful or **functional**. It is a unique art form that combines art, science, and nature.

Greening up a space can be as simple as planting some colorful flowers in a pot. It can also involve more planning and teamwork, such as starting an urban garden that provides the community with fresh food. Landscaping is big business, too. According to the National Gardening Survey in the United States, $36.1 billion was spent on lawns and gardens in 2015. In May 2016 alone, Canadians spent more than $769,000 on lawn-and-garden products.

GET OUTSIDE!

It pays to play outdoors. Time spent in the fresh air reduces stress, makes people more caring and sympathetic, improves critical-thinking skills, increases attention span, and makes it easier to maintain a healthy lifestyle. Fun, entertaining, and beautiful green spaces help draw us outside!

Make your dream landscape into a reality. Where will your creativity lead?

A MAKER MOVEMENT

The people who green up spaces are makers. They learn how to tackle any project through hands-on, real-world experience. Makers risk failure, but they keep working to find **innovative** solutions to problems. Landscapers are makers who create, build, and grow living masterpieces, both big and small.

Makers gather together in **makerspaces**. Here they share resources and knowledge, and work on projects. **Collaborative** workspaces allow for the sharing of ideas. Make your makerspace a green space!

GROWING GREEN

Orca K-8 School in Seattle, Washington, is filled with budding green thumbs. The school has an **organic** gardening program in which students learn about nutrition by cooking and eating what they grow. Extra herbs, vegetables, and fruits are shared with a local food bank, and food waste from the school cafeteria is made into **compost**.

The best way to learn about all things green is to roll up your sleeves and dig in!

Be a Maker!

Makers can create special places outdoors in any space—big or small! What appeals to you about your backyard or neighborhood park? Why do you think you prefer one green space over another?

GREAT LANDSCAPES

People have been greening up spaces for more than 3,000 years. Gardens in ancient Egypt were **formal** and **symmetrical** spaces. Early Italian gardens were built like open-air buildings. Everything was structured. Trees were **pruned** into artificial shapes called **topiary**. In the 1700s in England, there was a switch to a more natural, free-form look.

GREENING OF A CONTINENT

When Europeans traveled to North America, they brought their gardening styles along. Landscapers now had a choice of styles. Frederick Law Olmsted is often called the "father of American landscape **architecture**." He helped design New York City's Central Park and the Capitol grounds in Washington, D.C. Olmsted believed parks should be functional green spaces for public use. In 1900, his son taught the country's first course in landscape architecture at Harvard University.

A GARDEN BY ANY OTHER NAME

There are formal gardens, food gardens, water gardens, roof gardens, gardens for entertaining, and gardens for wildlife. Calming, Japanese-style **zen** gardens are made up of a large area of raked sand with a rock or two and a few plants. They are built on the idea that humans are part of nature.

In a zen garden, rocks symbolize mountains and raked sand represents water.

The Renaissance garden is inspired by the belief that humans are the masters of nature. The elaborate gardens at Château de Versailles in France include 250 acres (100 ha) of paths, flower beds, statues, and even a canal once used for gondola rides. British Columbia's Butchart Gardens was created on the site of an abandoned rock quarry. It now boasts more than 700 different **species** of plants.

The High Line is an elevated green space that stretches about 1.5 miles (2.4 km) above the busy streets of Manhattan in New York City. It is built on an old railway line.

GOING BIG

Houston, Texas, is the latest hotspot to watch when it comes to landscape design. Makers and shakers in the United States' fourth-largest city are going green. Once called a concrete wasteland, Houston is transforming itself with the development of connected **greenways** and redeveloped parks.

Be a Maker!

If you had to choose a landscape design, would it be formal or informal? Why? What appeals to you about this style? What elements of this design could you use in your own green space?

LOOKING AT TREES, SHRUBS, AND FLOWERS

Different areas across North America have different **climates**. Some plants grow better than others in colder temperatures. Areas are classified according to how low temperatures drop. These classifications are called hardiness zones. Gardeners need to know which plants will grow well in their zone. You will not find palm trees growing in Yukon or reindeer moss in the Arizona desert!

WHAT YOU NEED TO KNOW

The **diversity** of plant life can be mind-boggling, but there are some basics. Coniferous trees are evergreen and keep their needles during the winter. If you want privacy year-round, choose a coniferous tree, such as a fir or pine. Deciduous trees lose their leaves every fall. If you are designing for color and a changing landscape, choose a deciduous tree, such as an oak or aspen. **Perennial** plants grow and bloom year after year. Potted plants are often **annuals** such as petunias, impatiens, and pansies. These displays must be replanted each year.

Plant choices can be based on size, from tall trees to shrubs to flowers to short grass. They can be chosen for their color or their fragrance. Plants are sometimes chosen based on how fast they grow. Some landscapes have poor soil conditions or bad drainage, or too much sun or shade.

Selecting plants with a good mix of color, texture, and height adds interest to a landscape.

GET GLOWING!

Specific plants are well suited to these different environments. Glowing plants could soon be lighting up your backyard! One bioengineering company is taking apart the building blocks of plants, and reconstructing them in unique ways to make plants that glow like a nightlight! They are also working on fragrant mosses, blue roses, a mosquito-repelling ivy, and fast-growing lettuce. Landscapers will soon have a whole new array of plants for their designs.

Hardy vegetables such as cabbage and Brussels sprouts grow well in areas with colder climates.

Makers and Shakers

The Boreal Garden Project

North Caribou Lake is a First Nation community located in Northern Ontario. Most of the food eaten by the locals is wild game such as moose and beaver. Growing fresh vegetables in a colder climate is challenging. All produce had to be flown in to the remote community until 2015, when the Boreal Garden Project took root. With gardening supplies, a little fish compost, advice from an expert gardener, and plenty of community spirit, the residents of North Caribou Lake started their own **sustainable** garden. In 2016, the annual Hunter's Festival wrapped up with a feast of wild meat, and—for the first time ever—fresh vegetables grown in the community garden.

THINK LIKE A LANDSCAPER

Landscapers are masters of making a green space visually appealing and functional.

THE BASICS

One of the first things a landscaper must do is to think about how much space he or she has to work with. A massive plant on a tiny balcony might look cramped. A small **patio** in a big backyard might look overpowered by the space around it. Many designs begin with a **focal point** that draws the eye into the landscape. It could be a water feature, a statue, or a piece of furniture. Designs are built around this focal point.

WHAT IS ON YOUR WISH LIST?

Keep asking questions to design the perfect green space! Are you hoping to create a space where you can throw a football? Do you want a private space where you can relax? Are you looking to grow your own food? Do you want to attract wildlife into your green space?

Creative landscapers create pleasing landscapes that appear striking from more than one perspective.

A **xeriscape** is a landscape design that works well in dry areas. Plants that require less water, such as cacti, are often added to these green spaces.

QUESTIONS TO ASK!

Design is all about thinking critically about the landscape plan. Is there too much open space, or not enough? How much sun and shade does the area get? Does it drain well, or does it capture a lot of water? Will the plants fill the space or grow too big? How will the garden look in spring, summer, fall, and winter?

PLANNING AND PERSPECTIVE

Once you have determined your wish list, start making your plan. There are two ways to sketch out a landscape. A plan view is what you would see if you were looking down on a landscape from the sky. This drawing shows the shape and size of the landscape, as well as the overall arrangement of the features in relation to each other.

A perspective view is used to show three dimensions, and gives a feeling of how the space might look as you would see it when you are standing on the ground. It might be drawn from a walkway with an overhanging **trellis** and raised flower beds.

Be a Maker!

Pretend that you have an unlimited budget to create a design with plants, structures, and textures. Sketch a plan view of your green space on grid paper. What works well in your mind? What elements might be tricky to pull off?

GREENING UP SMALL SPACES

Some people do not have big backyards in which to create green landscapes. No need to worry—where there is a will, there is a garden!

CONTAINED!

Container gardening can be used to green up spaces big and small. These mini-gardens are easy to construct, and simple to move around and reorganize. They can be used to block unpleasant views on patios or simply fill the senses with color and fragrance.

UP WE GROW!

When you cannot go out, go up! Vertical gardens are perfect for super-small spaces. In a vertical garden, containers are stacked or hung to use wasted space. Container gardens can be filled with colorful petunias and other fresh annuals each year. They could also be filled with perennial evergreens such as ivy, or herbs such as sage and thyme.

Vertical green spaces add color and visual interest to the sides of buildings in urban areas.

Making a terrarium is a great way to practice landscape design on a small scale.

TINY WORLDS

A **terrarium** is a creative and easy way to green up an indoor space. These tiny gardens are usually created in glass containers. A layer of **charcoal** at the bottom helps with drainage, and helps keep the plants healthy. Open-air containers work best for plants that do not need lots of water, such as cacti. Closed terrariums hold in moisture for plants that grow in damp, shady places, such as ferns.

FAIRY NICE!

Fairy gardens are pint-sized gardens full of imagination! They can be planted in any type of container you choose, just make sure there are drainage holes. Fairy gardens work well on porches and balconies. Start by putting soil in your container, then add miniature plants of varying heights, shapes, and colors. Top off your creation with homemade accessories such as fairy homes and toadstools. Creativity rules in fairyland!

Be a Maker!

Container gardens can be made of wood, concrete, plastic, or even funky salvaged items such as old teacups, boots, wooden pallets, or toy trucks. A garden can be planted in an old coffee pot or mason jar. Have a look around your home or school. What might make a unique container for a small garden?

MAKE IT!
VERTICAL GARDEN

Vertical gardens take up little space and can be grown on balconies. This eco-friendly option reuses old plastic soda bottles.

● Prepare your soda bottles by carefully cutting out a 6-inch (15-cm) long by 3-inch (7.5-cm) wide rectangle on one side, to create an opening for the plants.

● Holding each bottle on a firm surface, carefully make a mark or a small hole midway along the short edge of the opening. Make sure everyone's fingers are out of the way. It should be about a ½ inch (1 cm) away from the large opening, so that the plastic does not tear.
● Make a similar mark on the opposite short edge.
● Mark two holes in the bottom of each bottle for drainage.
● Holding the bottle horizontally, mark two holes on the bottom, directly below the top two holes.
● Place the bottle on a firm surface and carefully poke holes through all of the marks.

- Tie a knot in the bottom of one of your lengths of string or wire, then thread a washer onto the string or wire. Thread the string or wire through the top and bottom holes of the soda bottle.
- Repeat the step with the second piece of string or wire. Make sure that the bottle stays level.

3

- Leave a 12-inch (30-cm) space, and add the second and then third bottles.
- Tie a knot in the bottom ends of string or wire and cut off any excess.
- Fill the bottles with soil and add seeds or plants.
- Tie together the two pieces of string or wire at the top of your vertical garden.
- Ask an adult to help you put your hook into a wall outside your home that you have permission to use. Hang up your vertical garden and enjoy it every day!

4

Make It Even Better!

What other objects can you think of that could be used in place of recycled plastic bottles? What factors would limit what can and cannot be used effectively? Besides a patio or balcony, where else could this type of vertical garden be used?

CONCLUSION

Take a look at your finished vertical garden. Would it be better to have a variety of distances between the bottles to allow different sizes of plants more space to grow? How easy is it to care for the garden? How important is it to have the right amount of soil in each bottle?

CARING FOR YOUR GREEN SPACE

Gardens do not happen on their own. They take work! From planting to pruning, watering to weeding—green spaces need attention.

GET WET!

Water is essential for all green spaces. Setting up an automatic watering system is a luxury that may be worth investigating. There are options for makers to design their own systems, such as an **Arduino**-powered system. Take your ideas to a local makerspace and ask for input from other green thumbs!

DOWN IN THE DIRT

Most gardens start with a layer of soil. Plants absorb from the soil many of the nutrients they need to grow. Compost can be mixed in with the soil to give plants even more nutrients. Research how to make your own compost from leftover food scraps and yard waste.

DEADHEAD!

Deadheading sounds bad, but it actually allows some plants to keep blooming. Deadheading means to remove the dying flowers from a plant. When flowers droop, the plant puts energy into producing seedheads instead of new flowers. Removing dying flowers channels the plant's energy back into producing new flowers instead.

Using a watering can instead of a sprinkler helps reduce the amount of water needed to care for your garden, and lets you target the plants you want to grow, not pesky weeds!

Brightly colored flowers help attract pollinators to a garden.

BUG OUT

Keeping pests that like to feast on plants out of the garden is a good idea. So is attracting **pollinators** that help plants grow fruit and seeds. Insecticides are toxic chemicals that are used to get rid of unwanted pests, but they can also affect pollinators. Planting marigolds in between your tomatoes will keep unwanted pests out of your garden and will not hurt helpful insects. This is called companion planting. Herbs such as rosemary, oregano, parsley, and thyme are also useful in fighting pests. Research other natural solutions to keep pests out of your green space.

WEED ME!

Can't see your garden through the weeds? Not only do weeds hide the beauty of a green space, they also crowd out the plants you want to grow. When you are weeding, make sure you remove the entire plant, including the root, so the weed does not grow back. Covering soil with a layer of **mulch** also reduces weeds.

Makers and Shakers

Jacob Schindler

In sixth grade, Jacob Schindler's (born 1994) science project investigated growing an invasive weed called kudzu on Mars. He continued experimenting with the stubborn plant. He discovered that helium killed kudzu, but did not hurt the other plants around it. The project changed to getting rid of kudzu on Earth. Schindler modified a drill to inject helium into the ground—making the weed disappear! Today, he is nicknamed "the Kudzu Kid."

MORE THAN PLANTS!

Stone walkways, **gazebos**, wooden decks—landscaping involves more than pretty flowers. Hard landscaping, or **hardscaping**, is the use of materials such as brick, wood, stone, and concrete in a landscape. Hardscaped areas are durable, and once an area is hardscaped, it does not need a lot of maintenance.

ROCK ON!

Adding hard, natural materials to a landscape provides a contrast to greenery. A large rock can be the focal point of a design. Smooth river stones can be placed around the edge of a garden to create a border. Use small pebbles to create a winding path through a fairy garden, or larger rocks to build a statue.

Contrasting colors and shapes add visual interest to rock borders.

PLAN A PATH OR A PATIO

Paths are links into a landscape. They can lead straight into a garden, or take visitors on an adventure as they curve through the space. Patios are defined hardscaped areas often made of brick or paving stones. Lead on to the stone fire pit! S'mores anyone?

TAKE A SEAT!

From swings to stumps to benches, seating provides a place to sit back, relax, and enjoy a green space. Metal, wood, concrete, and plastic are all popular materials for garden seats. What kind of seat will work best in your green space?

STYLISH STRUCTURES

Pergolas and gazebos provide shade. Arbors are structures that plants can grow along. Wooden archways are decorative features. Compost bins and tool sheds may be practical, but with the right design, they can fit nicely into any landscape. Backyard wood structures can be fun, too—from tree houses to play structures. Seating provides a spot to sit back, relax, and enjoy a green space. Consider ways you can add hardscaping touches to your green space.

This wooden structure provides a focal point for a green space, and also serves as a place to escape the sun!

Be a Maker!

Time for a field trip! With an adult, take a walk around your neighborhood. Observe places where hardscapes exist, such as a sidewalk or stone wall. How do these elements balance with the surrounding landscape? How might adding plants add to their appeal?

WATER FEATURES

The sight and sound of water is peaceful and soothing. Ponds, fountains, and waterfalls are popular additions to many green spaces.

SPLISH-SPLASH!

Moving water adds a dynamic element to a green space. For ponds, a plastic liner keeps the water contained. For fountains and waterfalls, a pump helps keep water moving. After the basics are covered, style, layout, and plant choices are wide open for makers. Small fountains can be created with stacked stones, old teapots spilling one onto another, or by putting a simple spout in the center of a ceramic pot. In small spaces, a pond in a pot can be effective. All you need is a container, a few water plants, and the hose!

Portable water fountains come in a variety of shapes, styles, and colors. They work well for small spaces and patios.

RAIN GAIN

Rain barrels and rain chains are two eco-friendly water features that can be added to a green space. A rain barrel collects water that can be used to give thirsty plants a drink. A rain chain can be used to channel water away from an area so it can be collected in a watering can or barrel. With a little imagination, functional features such as these can be incorporated into any garden design. Place a screen on top of a rain barrel to keep mosquitoes away.

Rain barrels can be wood, plastic, or metal. Choose the material that best suits your space.

Be a Maker!

Bird baths are simple and inexpensive options for including a water feature in a green space. Store-bought bird baths can be concrete or plastic, but makers have lots of other options to consider. Grab an extra terracotta pot and tray from the shed. Turn the pot upside down as a base and use the tray for the bath. You could also build a tripod with thick pieces of tree branches, and top it with a secondhand bowl.
Use your imagination!

MAKE IT!
RAIN CHAIN

Rain chains came from Japan. These decorative chains are used instead of a metal downspout to channel water from roofs to the ground. Traditionally made of copper, you can find them made with terracotta pots, metal buckets, or even old utensils. Rain chains are functional, pretty to look at, and easy to make!

YOU WILL NEED
- Wire cutters
- Drill
- Pliers
- Stiff, flexible wire, about 40 inches (100 cm) long
- Scissors
- Metal hook
- Around five metal or plastic containers, such as the plastic cups used in this activity
- Watering can
- Mosquito netting
- Tape

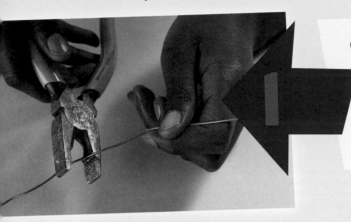

● Cut a piece of wire about 40 inches (100 cm) long with your wire cutters. Use the pliers to make a loop in one end. You will hang your rain chain from this loop.

1

2

● Ask an adult to help you drill a small hole in the bottom of each container. You will also need to drill a hole in the side of the container near the top, as shown in this photo.

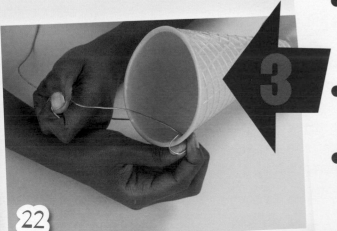

3

● Pull the end of the wire through the hole at the top of one container. Leave the loop at the top. Thread the wire through the hole in the bottom of the container.

● Repeat step 3 with the wire and the rest of your containers, until you have made a chain.

● Bend the bottom of the wire into a U-shape about 1½ inches (4 cm) long, then twist it 2–3 times to create a loop. This will hold the final container in place.

4 Now find a place you want to hang your rain chain. You can hang it from a building. Or you could hang it from the base of a tree branch. Screw your hook into wherever you want to hang the rain chain from, then attach the loop from step 1 to the hook.

5 Finally, place your watering can beneath the rain chain. Make sure that you cover the top with a screen to keep mosquitoes from breeding in the water. Be sure to tape it securely in place.

Make It Even Better!

What natural containers could you use instead of plastic containers to make a rain chain? What recycled household items could you use? How might you change your rain chain to reflect the seasons?

CONCLUSION

Take time to watch your rain chain in action. How well does your rain chain work in heavy rain? What could you do to make it stronger and more durable? Where else could you hang your rain chain?

THE EDIBLE LANDSCAPE

Make a garden and grow your own food! It is cheaper than buying vegetables from a store, environmentally-friendly, and sustainable. Greening up spaces can turn tasty when you plant your favorite fruits, vegetables, and herbs!

DIGGING INTO HISTORY

Native peoples developed the practice of growing corn, beans, and squash together. These plants are called the "three sisters" and they are companion plants. Beans produce nitrogen, which helps the corn and squash grow. Corn provides a tall stalk on which beans climb. Squash provide ground cover which helps keep the soil moist. Do some research and plan your vegetable patch so that the plants can benefit from one another, too!

Lettuce grows well with carrots, but not so well with parsley. Companion planting involves planting certain types of plants next to each other to improve yield and to gain other benefits.

A BLOOMING IDEA

Fannie Griscom Parsons (1850–1923) was a New Yorker who started one of the first children's gardens in the United States in 1902. She wanted kids to have a beautiful place to gather and to grow food. Today, City Blossoms follows in the footsteps of Fannie and the Victory Gardens by developing creative, kid-driven urban gardens in Washington, D.C., Baltimore, and Philadelphia. In the Mighty Greens program, high-school students pair their green thumbs with business skills. After harvesting the vegetables, the produce is sold in the local community. It is also used to make soap and lotion. Is there a community garden in your neighborhood? If not, gather some friends and start one!

UP ON THE ROOFTOP

In New York City, the Brooklyn Grange is a 40,000-square-foot (3,716-sq-m) farm on top of a building in the Brooklyn Navy Yard. The farm has a second location on Long Island. Together, the two farms produce about 50,000 pounds (22,700 kg) of food each year. If you do not have enough backyard space for an edible landscape, try thinking outside the box about other places to grow a garden.

Special strawberry pots save space and increase the amount of fresh fruit produced. These pots can also be used to grow a variety of fresh herbs.

Makers and Shakers

Hart Fogel

In 2015, 16-year-old Hart Fogel (born 1999) won an award for his work in creating a Marin City community garden. California has a youth court where young people in trouble with the law choose to be sentenced by their peers. Hart has been involved with this program in Marin County since seventh grade. The garden is a place where young offenders can serve community service hours. Fresh food and a fresh start!

GOING WILD!

Natural habitats in many urban areas are rare. Some people like to garden for the birds, bees, and all kinds of other wildlife. Picking the right plants can attract certain species to your yard. All animals need food, water, and shelter to survive. If you can offer this in your green space, they will come.

WHAT MAKES A GOOD WILDLIFE GARDEN?

Different species have different food and shelter needs. A variety of spaces and places is most effective for attracting the greatest diversity of wildlife. Water, even simple bird baths always attracts wildlife.

Consider adding plants that offer food year-round. Nectar, pollen, berries, and seeds are food sources for many different insects and birds. Sunflowers are nature's bird feeders. Growing a few plants in your garden will feed birds in the fall. If food plants are in short supply in winter months, make a bird feeder to hold seeds. You can also take old onion bags and fill them with **suet**, which is a favorite food for chickadees, woodpeckers, nuthatches, jays, and wrens.

Boil one part sugar and four parts water together, then let the liquid cool. Fill and hang a couple of feeders to attract tiny hummingbirds.

Birds like the shelter of a thick patch of trees or shrubs. Make a few nesting boxes and secure them in sheltered locations. Research the type of birdhouse the birds in your area prefer. Tall grasses are used for nesting material. Dead trees attract birds that like to nest in holes. They also provide shelter for many species of insects.

GOING BATTY

Bat boxes are easy to build and can attract these fascinating animals to your backyard. Bats are sometimes given a bad rap, but they are fantastic insect-eaters. A single little brown bat can eat up to 1,000 mosquitoes in one hour! Bat boxes are narrow and have an opening at the bottom that the animals can fly in and out through.

With some scrap wood, a hammer, and some nails, it is easy to build a bat box that gives these animals a safe, cozy place to sleep during the day.

Be a Maker!

Naturescapes are natural landscapes that are good for the environment. Why do you think that is true? What species would you like to attract to your backyard? Do some research to find out what plants and foods are best suited for this purpose.

MAKE IT!
BUTTERFLY GARDEN

There are more than 700 species of butterflies in the United States, and close to 300 known species in Canada. Make a butterfly garden for the butterflies in your area!

- Start by researching butterfly species in your area. Read up on what kinds of flowers attract these winged beauties. Bright flowers and nectar-rich flowers are a good place to start.

- Plan out your butterfly garden. Sketch out a design on grid paper, or use an app or software to lay out the design. Include where you will place the different flowers and other features. Think about the visual appeal of the space, too. Gather all your supplies.

- Fill the planter with potting soil. Use a small trowel to dig holes for each plant. Make sure each flower has room to grow. Place the flowers in the holes. Gently press the soil down around the base of each plant. Water each flower.

With a knife, carefully slice up an orange and banana into small pieces. Place the fruit on a saucer. Add a second dish with a little bit of water and sand in it.

- Set a flat rock in the planter as a resting place for the butterflies. Place the saucers on the rock.
- Place the planter in your garden or a space in your backyard.
- Take care of your garden. Water and weed on a regular basis. Replace the fruit and water every day or two. Then, sit back and watch the beautiful butterflies visit your garden!

Make It Even Better!

What plants could you add to your planter to attract other animals, such as pollinators? Where could you find plants and/or seeds without having to buy them? How would you create a garden that starts small and grows over the years?

CONCLUSION

Observe your garden several times a day over the course of a week. What kinds of butterflies were attracted? What time of day seemed to be the busiest? How does the amount of sunlight affect activity? How could you adjust the amount of shade your garden receives?

GLOSSARY

annuals Plants that complete their life cycle in one year

architecture The art and science of designing public spaces and structures

Arduino A company dealing with computer hardware and software

charcoal An absorbent, black material

climates Particular weather patterns in a region

collaborative Produced by two or more people working together

compost Plant material that decays and is used to improve soil

diversity Variety

focal point An element that draws the eye

formal Arranged in an orderly manner

functional Useful

gazebos Garden shelters that have sloped roofs

greenways Strips of land near urban areas that are usually set aside for recreation

innovative Original and creative

makerspaces Places where makers meet to share ideas, innovate, and invent

mulch Ground covering of plant material used to reduce weeds and retain moisture

Native Describing people, animals, or plant species that have always lived in a specific area

organic Grown naturally without chemicals

patio A flat seating area, usually covered with brick or stone

perennial A plant that lives for more than two years

pergolas Wooden or metal frame structures which can be used to support plants or provide light shade

pollinators Animals such as insects that move pollen from one plant to another

pruned To have cut off unwanted branches

species One of the groups into which plants are divided

suet Hard, white fat from animals

sustainable Done in a way that can be continued

symmetrical To be balanced or the same on both sides of a line or around a central point

terrarium A clear vessel used to grow plants indoors

topiary The art of clipping shrubs or trees into ornamental shapes

trellis A framework of thin metal or wood strips that cross each other

zen Reflective and peaceful

LEARNING MORE

BOOKS

Amstutz, Lisa J. *Enchanted Gardening: Growing Miniature Gardens, Fairy Gardens, and More.* Capstone Press, 2016.

Dyer, Hadley. *Potatoes on Rooftops: Farming in the City.* Annick Press, 2012.

Heinecke, Liz Lee. *Outdoor Science Lab for Kids: 52 Family-Friendly Experiments for the Yard, Garden, Playground, and Park.* Quarry Books, 2016.

Krezel, Cindy. *Kids' Container Gardening: Year-Round Projects for Inside and Out.* Chicago Review Press, 2010.

WEBSITES

Discover how to build a community through greening and gardening:
https://communitygarden.org

Kids Gardening is the place to learn about gardening with hands-on activities and educational resources:
www.kidsgardening.org

PBS Crafts for Kids shows how to build a succulent (plants that require little water) container garden:
www.pbs.org/parents/crafts-for-kids/diy-succulent-container-garden

The Canadian and American governments have plant hardiness maps. Find them at:
www.planthardiness.gc.ca
http://planthardiness.ars.usda.gov/PHZMWeb

INDEX

ABOUT THE AUTHOR

Megan Kopp is the author of more than 70 books for young readers.
She loves rock gardens, ponds, and natural landscaping for wildlife.